Best of luck from
Jim + Joni @ associated

W9-AVT-447

WISCONSIN

Aerial photography by Larry Mayer
Foreword by Tommy G. Thompson
Captions by Richard J. Wesnick

American & World Geographic Publishing and

La Crosse Tribune • Wisconsin State Journal and The Capital Times, Madison • The Journal Times, Racine

WISCONSIN
from the sky

Above: Looking like an eerie landscape painting, farms and ridges poke out above a fog bank east of La Crosse.

Title page: Fall colors explode along the shoreline of Stockton Island, among the islands of Apostle Islands National Lakeshore in Lake Superior.

Half title page: An autumn rain shower embellishes forests and farms north of Wausau.

Write for our catalog: American & World Geographic Publishing, P. O. Box 5630, Helena, Montana 59604

Printed in USA on Wisconsin-made paper.

Library of Congress Cataloging-in-Publication Data
Mayer, Larry.
   Wisconsin from the sky / aerial photography by Larry Mayer ; Foreword by Tommy G. Thompson.
     p.   cm.
   ISBN 1-56037-057-2
   1. Wisconsin--Aerial photographs.   I. Title.
   F582.M39   1994
   917.75'0022'2--dc20   94-18203

FOREWORD

From the sky, it becomes readily apparent that Wisconsin is a land of diversity—both in its landscape and in its people.

The Chippewa Indians called the state "Ouisconsin"—land of the gathering of the waters. With more than 1,000 miles of Great Lakes and Mississippi River shoreline, nearly 15,000 glacial lakes and thousands of miles of rivers and streams, it is a fitting name.

Wisconsin is still the land of rolling forestland, rugged landscape and rich prairieland inhabited by native American tribes thousands of years ago and later by Europeans of all ethnic backgrounds.

It is a land of red barns and patchwork fields, bluffs and beaches, tree-lined slopes and winding rivers, bustling cities and quaint villages.

It is a land of cheese and milk, sweet corn and cranberries.

It is a land of progressive, clean and open government.

It is a land of blossom-filled springs, green and lush summers, brilliant autumns and snowy winters.

It is a land of friendly and hard-working people whose warm hospitality is legendary.

"A noble land of good fields and magnificent trees, a gentleman's countryside, neat and white fenced," wrote author John Steinbeck, "a variety of field and hill, forest and lake."

Wisconsin's landscape reminded immigrants of home when they settled here during the 19th century. They chose their townsites carefully and christened them with such names as Luxembourg, Pulaski, Cedarburg and New Glarus.

For more than 150 years, the patchwork quilt of Old World culture has lived, worked and prospered in Wisconsin. Milwaukee, the state's largest city, perhaps does the most in capitalizing on its roots with many ethnic festivals, neighborhoods and restaurants. Madison also represents a cultural diversity centering on the noted University of Wisconsin and the state Capitol.

Wisconsin is a perfect combination of many of the good things in life: fresh air and fun, cities and country, old and new, and most importantly, some of the most friendly and warm people in the world.

Today, Wisconsin lures visitors with the slogan "You're Among Friends." And a trip through its lush countrysides, intimate villages and friendly cities will make any visitor feel as though they never left home.

—Governor Tommy G. Thompson

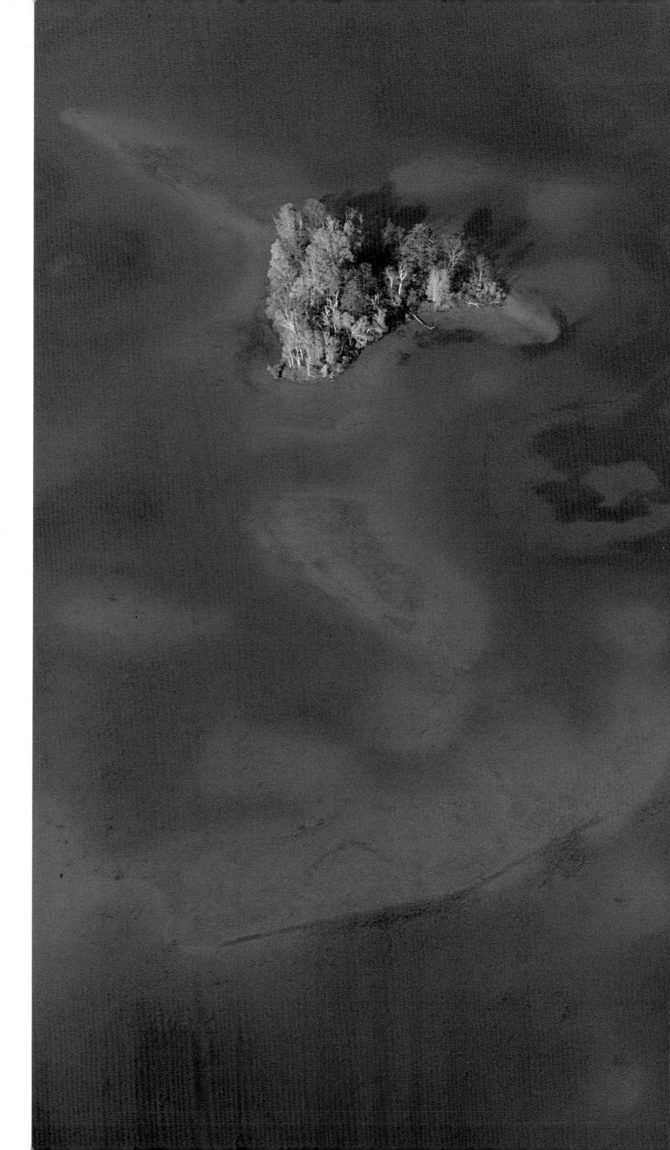

Standing like coral reefs in the Caribbean, small islands rise in Mackaysee Lake on Chambers Island, northern Green Bay.

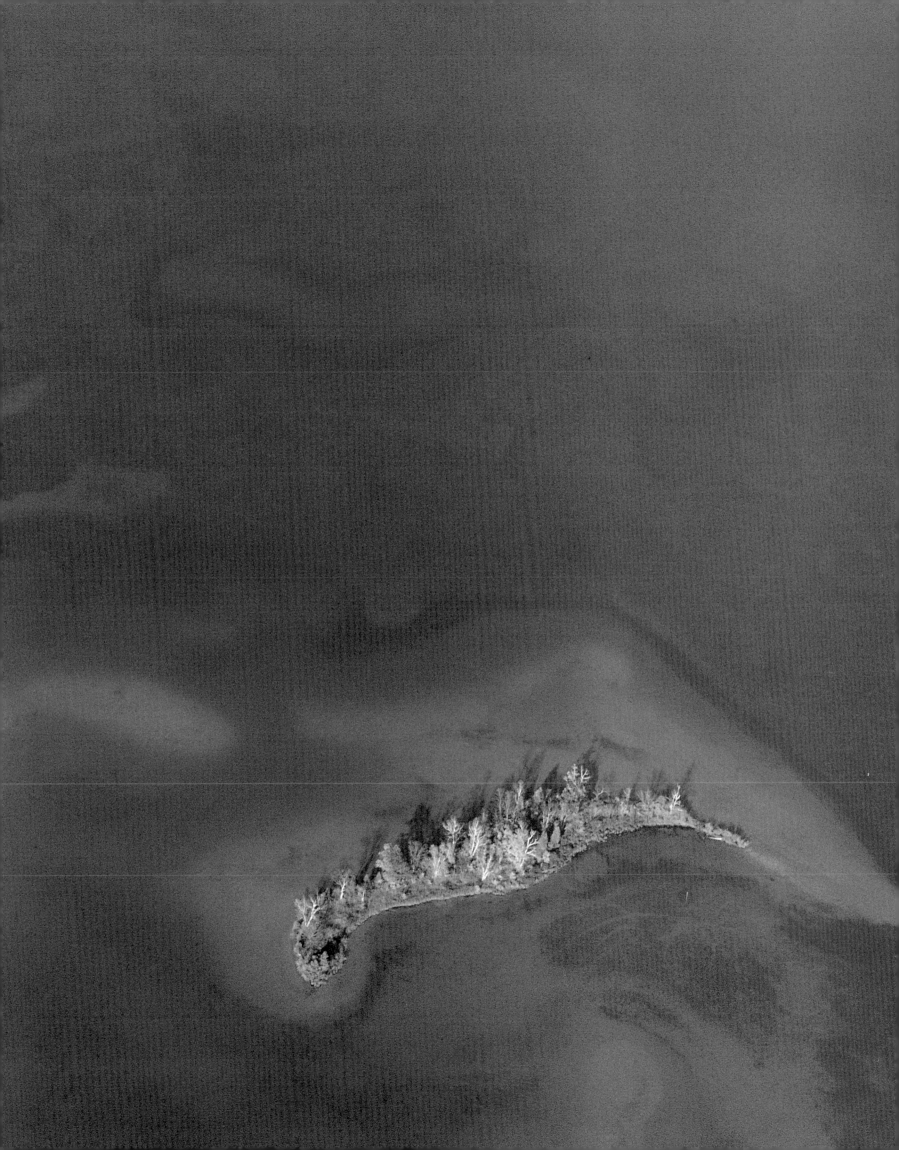

Left: A dazzling new marina marks Racine harbor, where lakeshore convention facilities, condos, a restaurant with a breathtaking view and other amenities have transformed the once-neglected lakefront into the new healthy heart of the city.

Facing page: Highway 35 makes up part of the Great River Road, a 250-mile scenic drive along the Mississippi River. It is a favorite route for motorists following the fall color tour. This scene is just south of Lock and Dam No. 9 in Crawford County.

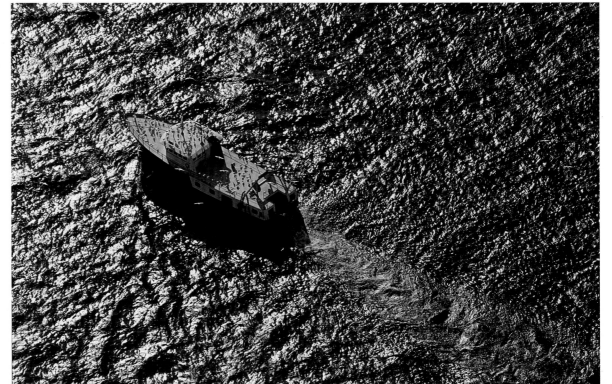

A fishing boat cuts through light chop on Green Bay as the sun dances off the tops of the waves.

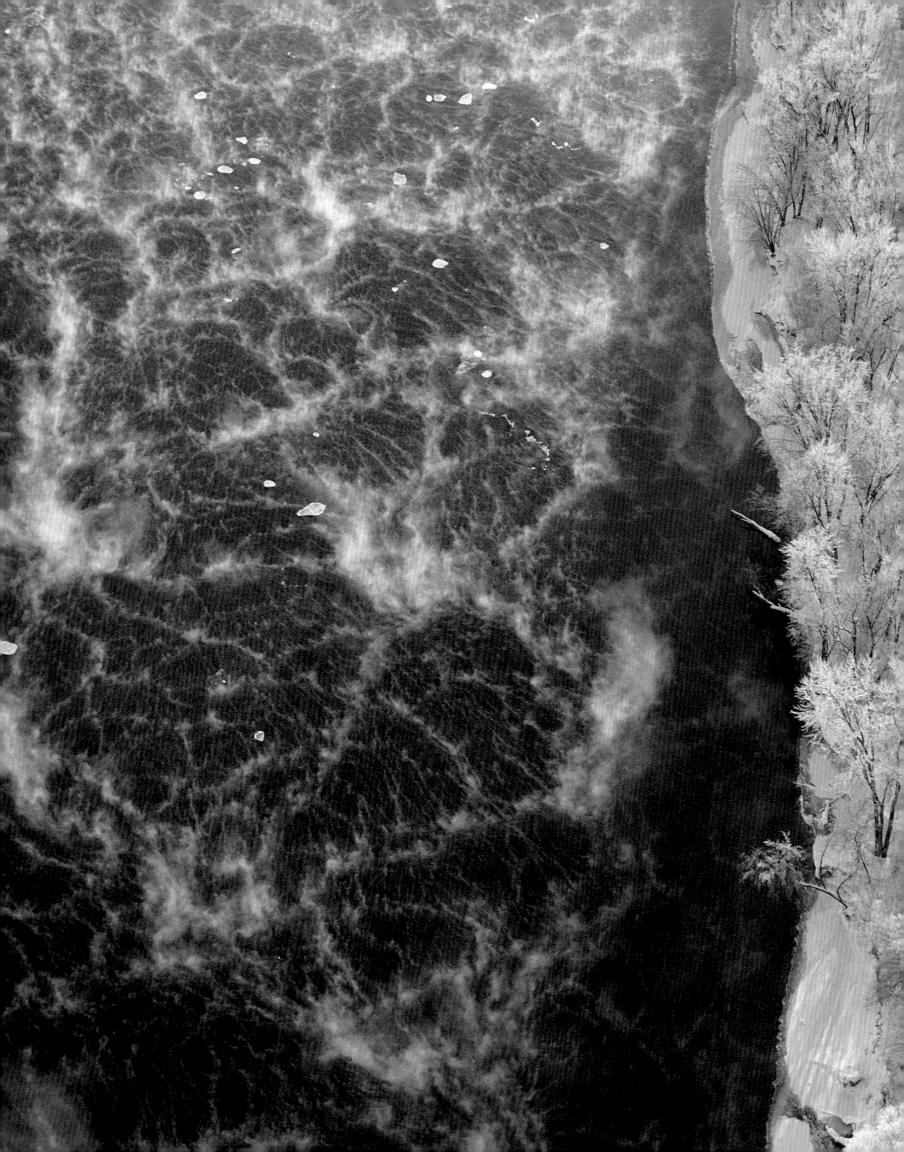

Above: Tugs break channels through the ice in Sturgeon Bay to keep the waterway open to shipping traffic.

Left: A heavy winter frost along the shores of the Wisconsin River near Mosinee.

Overleaf: The brilliant blue waters of Nelson Lake stand out against the rainbow of autumn color in the surrounding forests. Nelson Lake near Hayward is but one of the thousands of lakes that dot Wisconsin's north country.

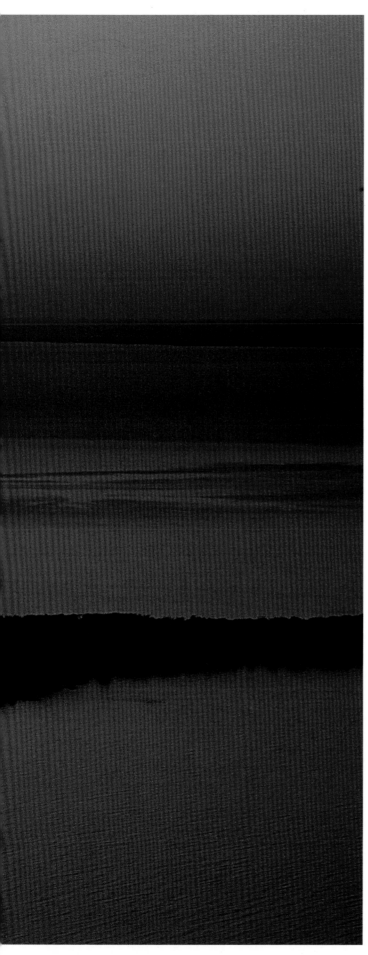

A blazing orange sunset sweeps over Door County's Little Sturgeon, Riley's and Sand bays. Door County is one of Wisconsin's many popular vacation destinations, with state parks, campgrounds, marinas and towns that hint of Cape Cod.

Right: Nature's potholes, carved by glaciers and weather, dot the landscape near Drummond in Bayfield County below Lake Superior.

Above: Lake Winnebago provides a beautiful backdrop for Oshkosh, city of industry and parks.

Right: This barn near Stevens Point demonstrates the pride Wisconsin residents have in their state.

Facing page: Drifting fog settles into the lowlands near Prairie du Sac.

Facing page: The low winter sun drags long shadows from farm buildings across snow-covered fields southeast of Wausau.

Left: Moonlight bathes Milwaukee at dusk.

Landscape as green as Ireland engulfs one of the idyllic farms near Chequamegon Bay on Lake Superior.

Overleaf: Sunrise sweeps across the Apostle Islands in Lake Superior.

21

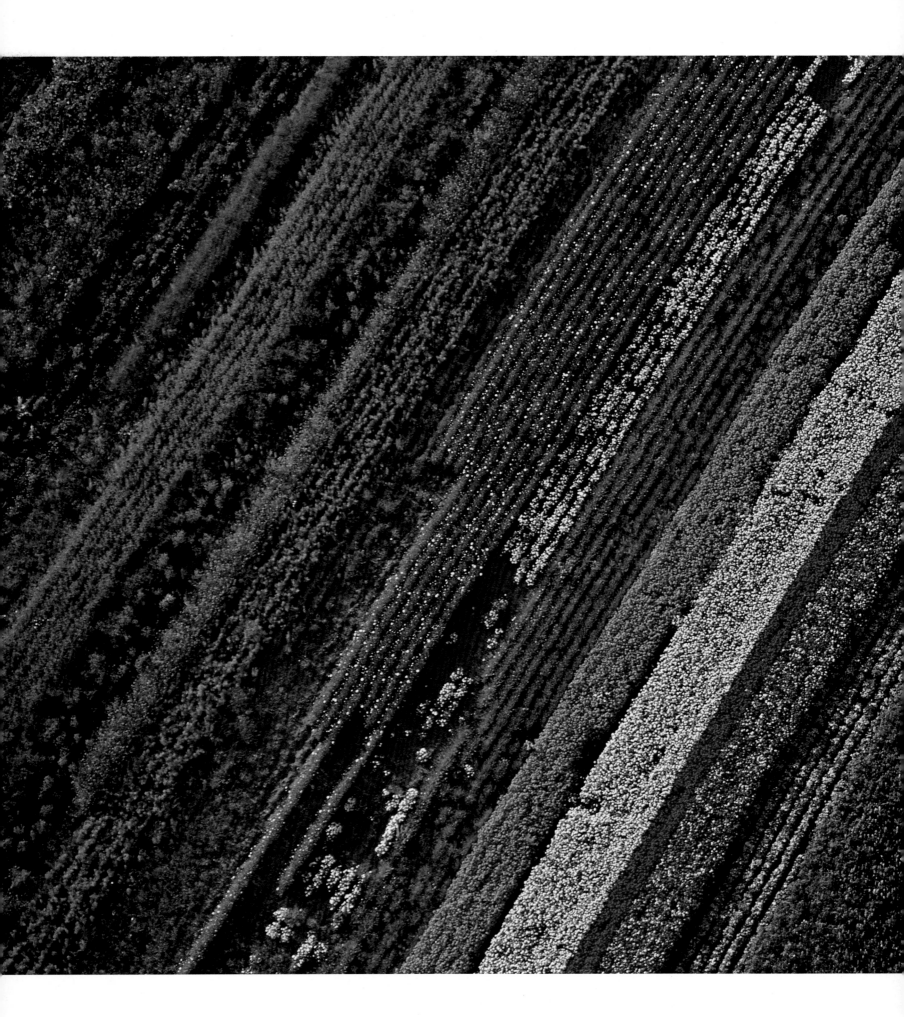

Rows of commercially grown flowers paint the fields near Bayfield in rich, vibrant colors.

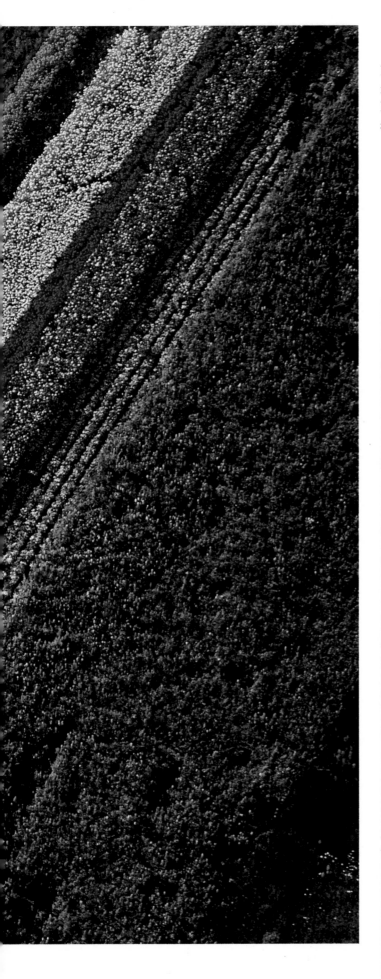

Below: Frank Lloyd Wright's Hillside Home School at Spring Green represents some of the famed architect's finest work. Tours of the National Historic Landmark include the Dana Gallery, Robert's Room, a theater and a drafting studio.

Right: Rib Mountain, the second highest point in Wisconsin, rises just beyond Wausau.

Below: Cruising across a water-lovers' paradise on the Mississippi River.

Facing page: The spires of one of the most magnificent Catholic churches in the country—a Carmelite shrine to Mary, Help of Christians—reach toward the sky from atop Holy Hill in Washington County, northwest of Milwaukee. The shrine each year is visited by thousands of people of all faiths who revel in its serenity, beauty and spectacular vistas.

Following spread: Farm fields form natural sculptures as they follow the contours of the land through the hills northwest of Lone Rock in Richland County.

Above: A farmer works to beat winter as he harvests the last of his corn crop near Burlington.

Right: Each winter, small temporary communities crop up on Wisconsin's many inland lakes. These ice shanties are on Big Eau Pleine Reservoir near Mosinee.

Facing page: The Wisconsin state capitol juts above the skyline of Madison, one of the most beautiful capital cities in America. Lakes Mendota and Monona surround Madison to provide year-round recreation.

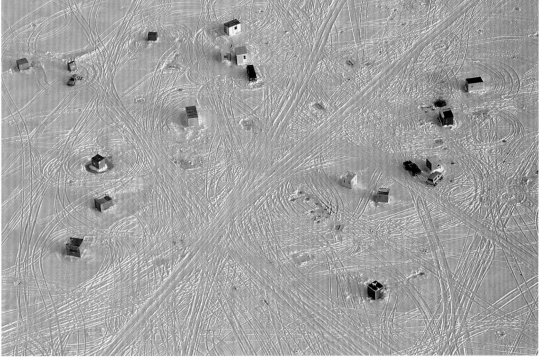

The Wisconsin River snakes its way through snow-covered hills and fields north of the town of Wisconsin Rapids.

Tens of thousands pack Camp Randall Stadium in Madison for a University of Wisconsin football game. The UW Badgers had one of their greatest seasons in history in 1993 and won the Rose Bowl on New Year's Day, 1994.

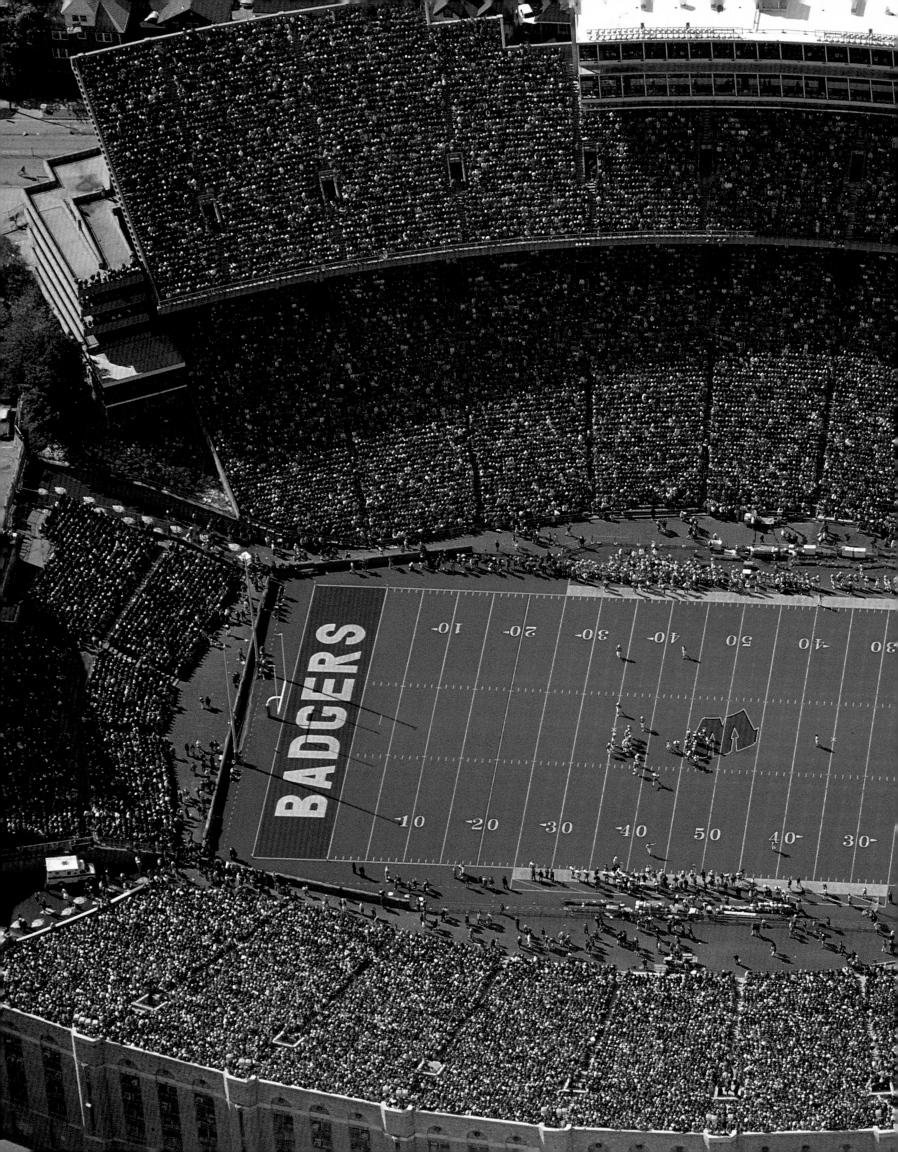

Camp Randall Stadium in Madison is awash in the red and white colors of the University of Wisconsin during a homecoming game against Northwestern University.

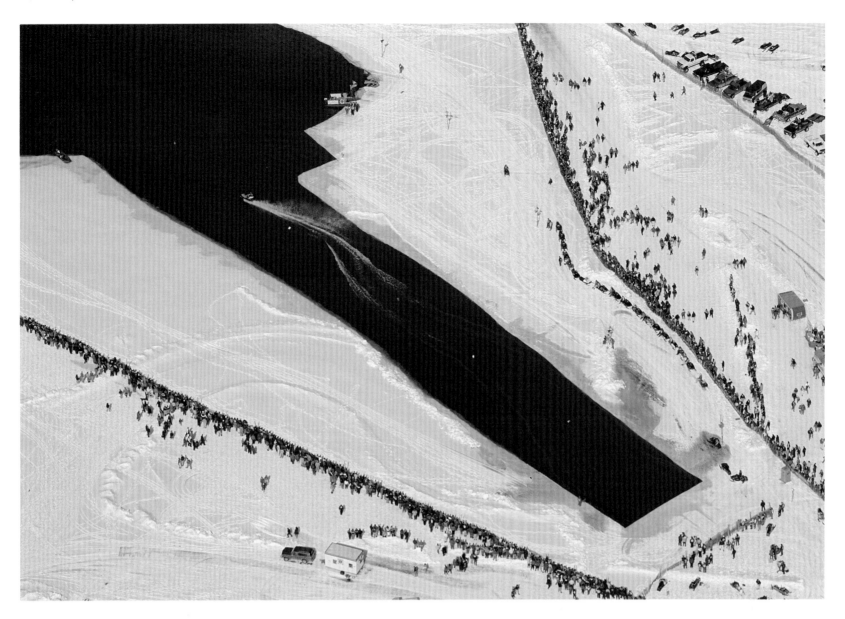

Facing page: Clam Lake in Burnett County turns into an ice-covered parking lot as spectators line up hundreds of cars to watch races in which snowmobiles race across the ice and try to "skip" open patches of water.

Top: It takes a considerable amount of sheer nerve and an enormous amount of sheer power to take part in snowmobile skip races at Siren. The machines roar across the open water, to the cheers of the crowd, as far as their power will take them.

Left: A snow and ice-covered wilderness spans the countryside as winter tightens its grip on the lakes and forests south of Rhinelander.

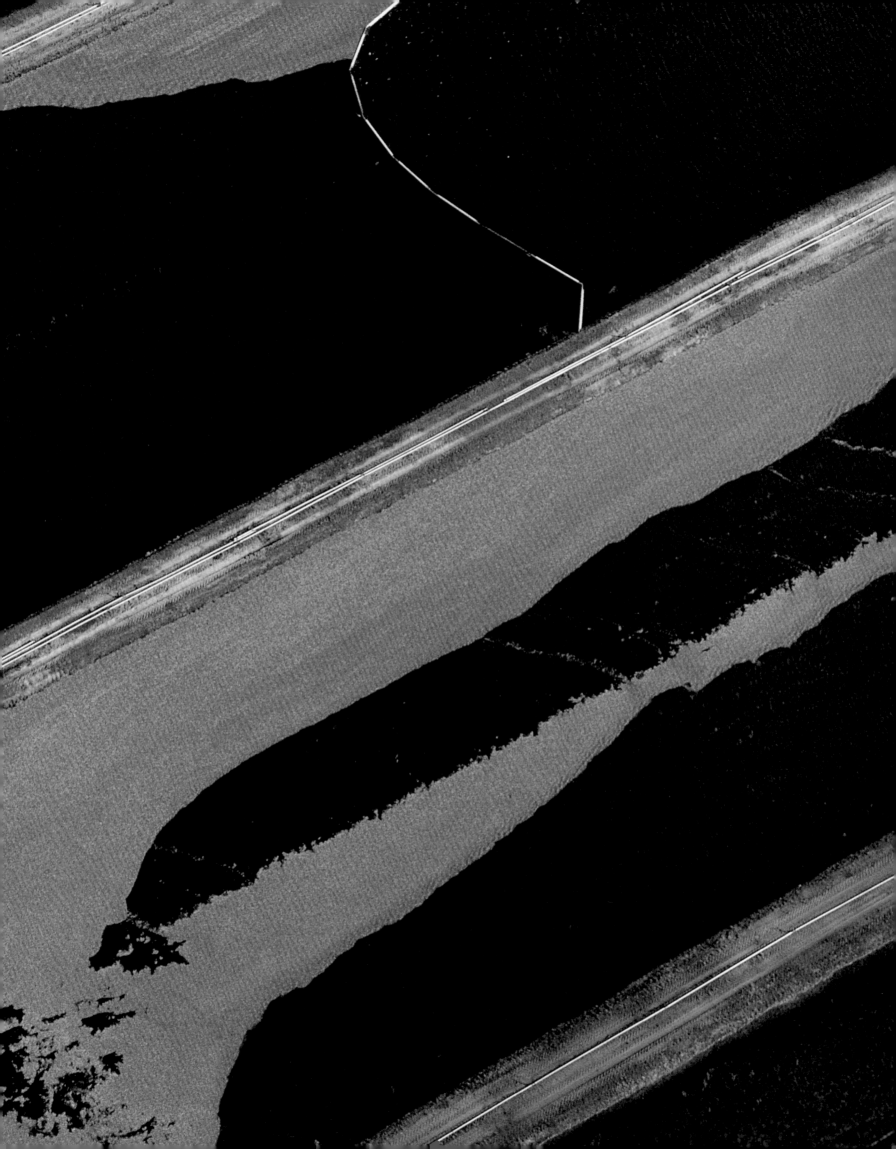

It doesn't get much better than this—night baseball at Milwaukee County Stadium, home of the Milwaukee Brewers.

Preceding spread: The waters run red with the fruit of the harvest when it's cranberry time in the bogs near Three Lakes, between Eagle River and Rhinelander.

The daring and the tranquil meet on Lake Geneva in southern Walworth County.

There's no business like the fun business in Wisconsin Dells, the fun capital of the world. Waterslides and tidal wave swimming pools are among many recreational and tourist activities that draw tens of thousands of people to Wisconsin Dells each year.

La Crosse, a city that grew up on the banks of the Mississippi, is a growing, bustling community that takes great pride in its unique beauty.

Overleaf: Corn fields create a harvest-time zig-zag pattern near Juda in Green County east of Monroe.

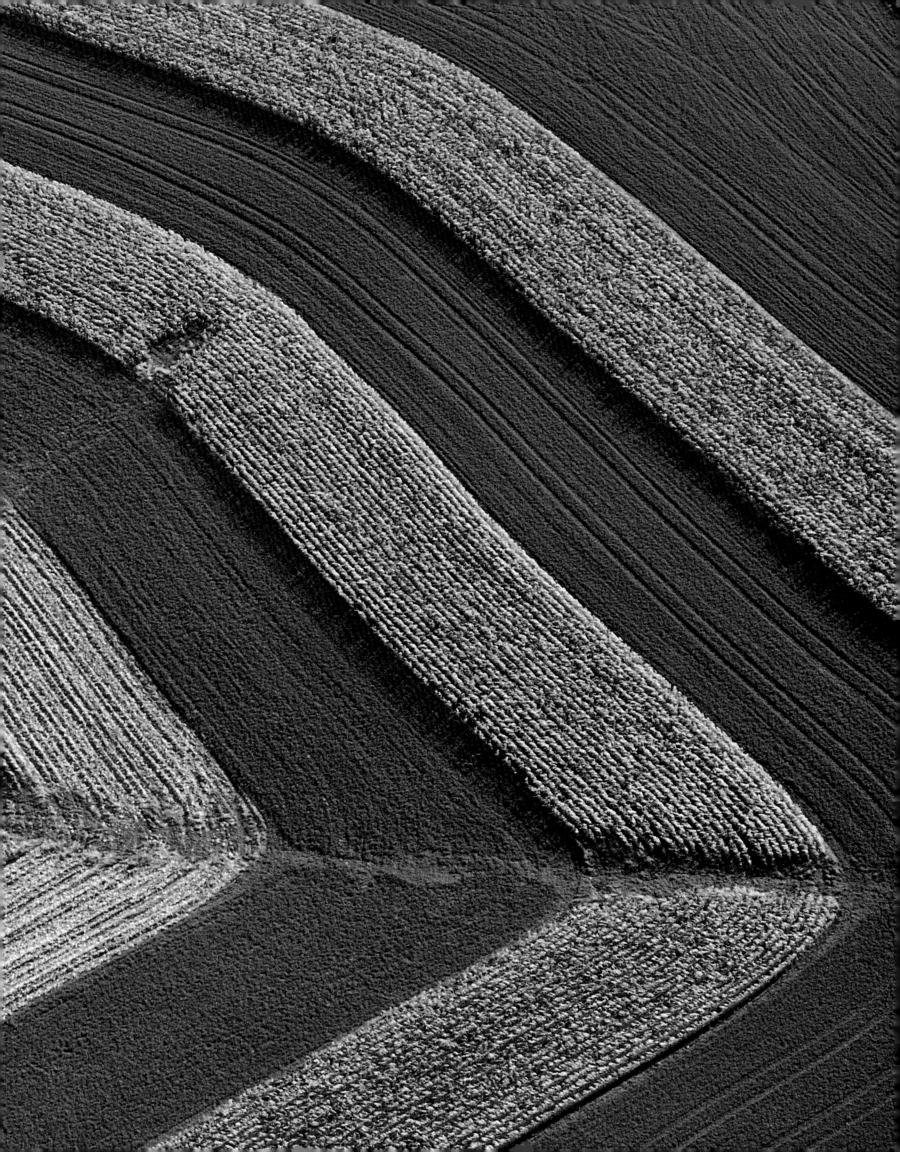

Right: A steam engine from the Mid-Continent Railway Museum threads through autumn fields at North Freedom, west of Baraboo.

Below: Farm fields chiseled out of the multi-colored forests near Wausau.

The community
of La Pointe on
Lake Superior's
Madeline Island is
accessible by ferry
boat from Bayfield
in summer, or by
the ice road across
the frozen straits in
winter.

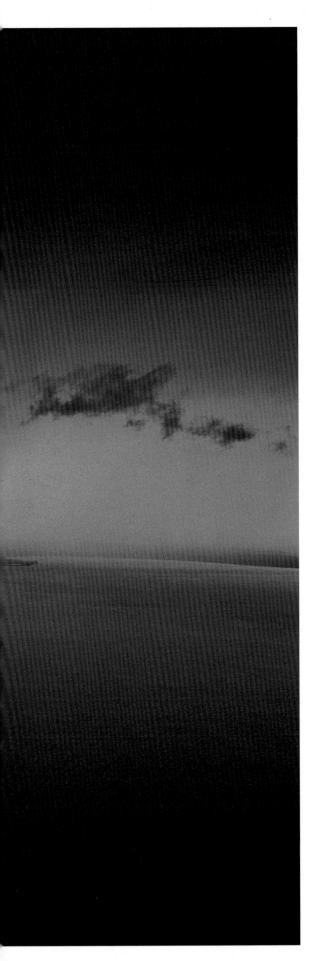

Left: Rainy skies over Pentenwell Lake south of Wisconsin Rapids.

Above: Cave Point reaches out into Lake Michigan from Whitefish Dunes State Park in Door County.

Overleaf: A loader stacks rows of logs at the Wausau Paper Mills Company plant at Brokaw just north of Wausau.

Above: Clouds cast mottled shadows across the Lake Michigan shoreline near Kewaunee.

Right: Picturesque rural communities such as Eastman near the Mississippi River in Crawford County are the mainstay of Wisconsin.

Far right: Highway 2 west of Ashland turns into a ribbon of gold under the setting summer sun.

Preceding spread: A brilliant sunrise glistens off the waters of Willow Reservoir in western Oneida County.

Facing page: Sailboats by the score stand at anchor in the Milwaukee harbor. Lake Michigan, one of Wisconsin's greatest natural resources, provides a wealth of water sports.

Right: Neillsville in Clark County, shrouded under an early morning fog.

Below: The East meets the West in Wisconsin, where soybeans are raised for soy sauce and where—as at this farm in Marathon County—you may find a crop of ginseng.

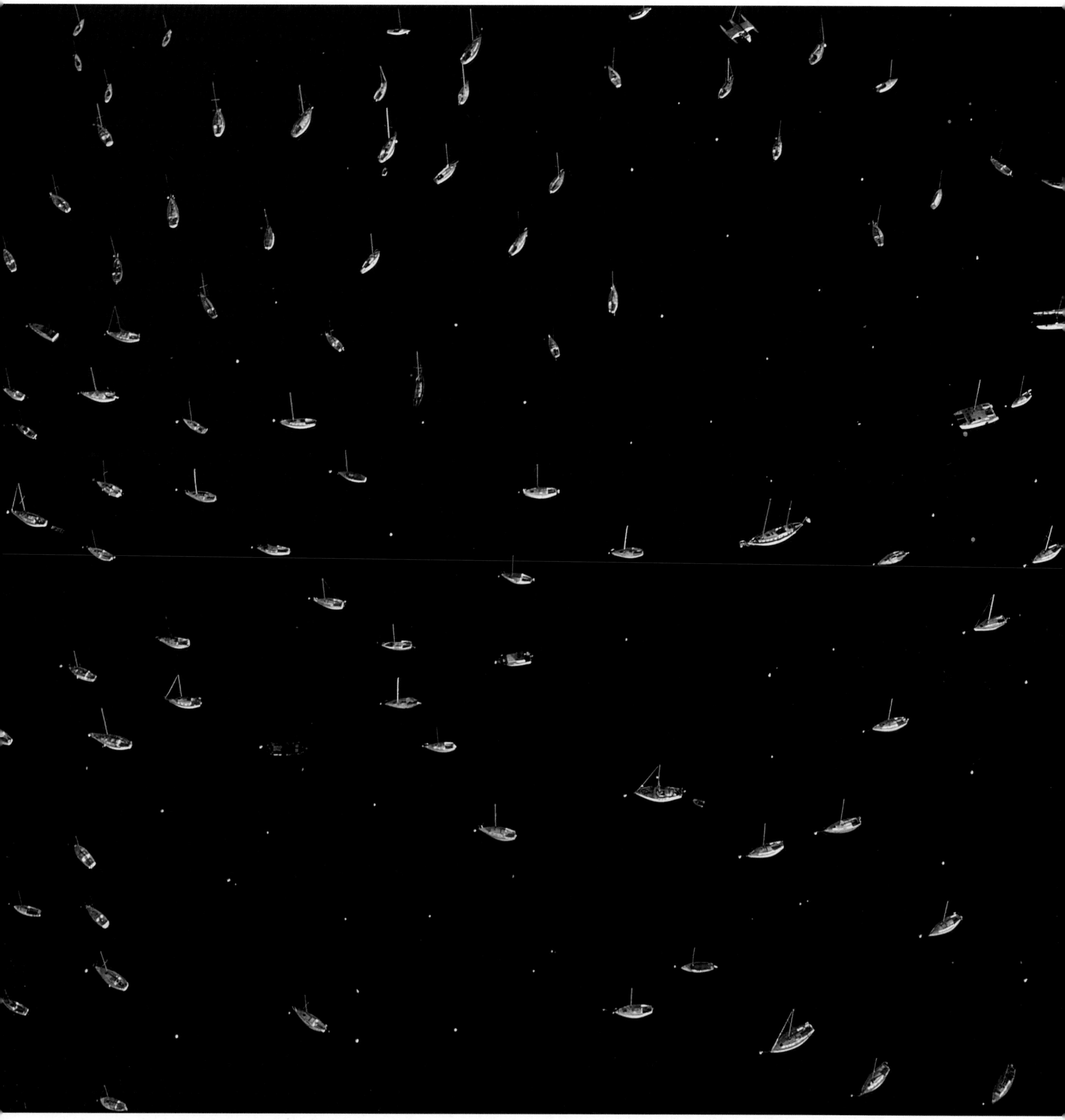

Preceding spread: Leaf-bare and snow-covered, a forest near La Crosse is locked in the grips of winter.

Right: Wausau pilot Glen Witter flies his Boeing PT-17 Stearman to the Experimental Aircraft Association airshow in Oshkosh. The annual summer airshow attracts thousands of aircraft of every shape and description, as well as tens of thousands of visitors.

Below: A snowstorm sweeps across the skies near Tomahawk.

Left: The city of Bayfield offers a spectacular view of Lake Superior. It is a jumping off point for Madeline Island and the Apostle Islands via cruise service and ferry boat. Bayfield also offers The Cooperage Museum with exhibits on the history of barrel-making.

Below: The lookout tower at the north end of Quincy Bluff commands a vast panorama, from the Wisconsin River where it pours out of Castle Rock Lake in the west, to the rolling hills, moraines, fields and forests of Adams County.

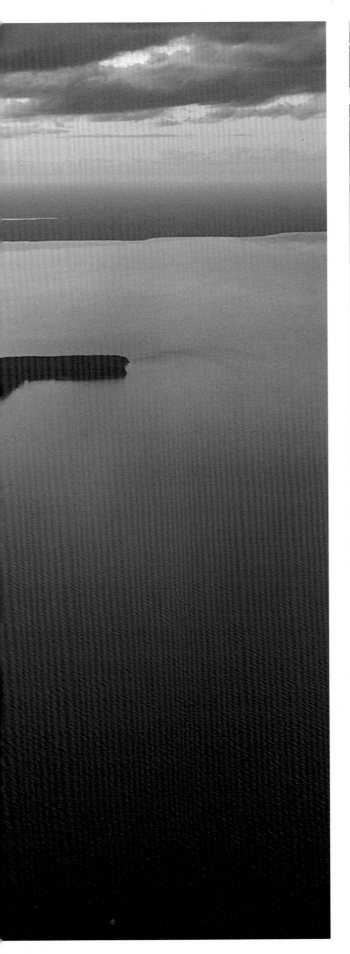

Above: When the snow flies, the skiers head for Rib Mountain near Wausau, one of Wisconsin's many popular ski resorts.

Left: Sunset spills a palette of color over a tranquil Green Bay where it wraps around Chambers Island.

Facing page: Forests along the Willow River west of Rhinelander float above the fog.

Left: The St. Croix National Scenic Riverway near Grantsburg separates two states, Wisconsin on the right and Minnesota on the left.

Below: Winter brings solitude and beauty to a cemetery at Madison.

Overleaf: Gleaming white buildings and a bright red barn east of La Crosse are symbolic of Wisconsin's rich agricultural heritage.

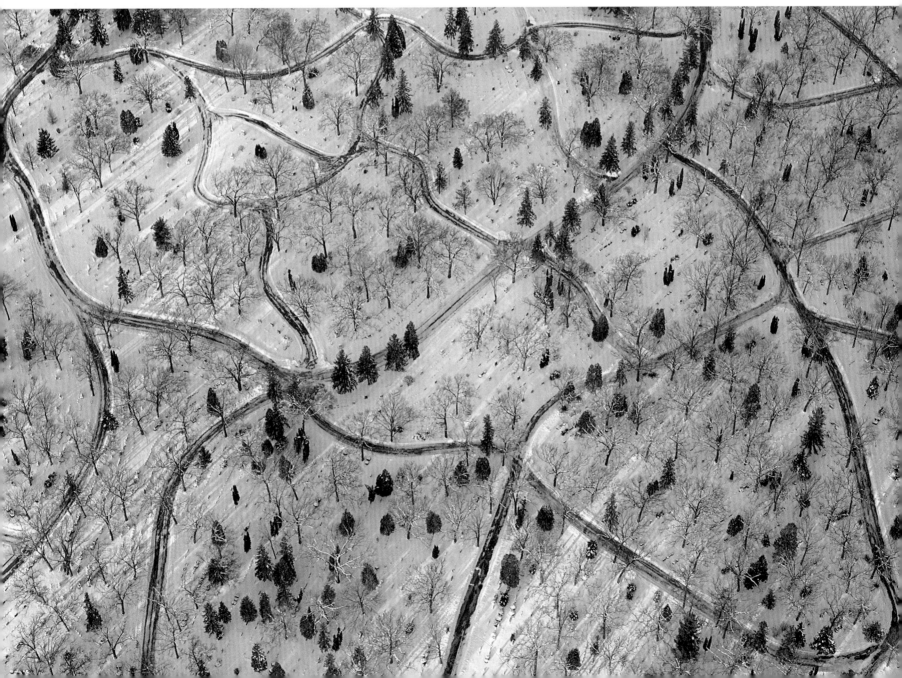

Right: Kenosha, located along the shores of Lake Michigan between Racine and the Illinois state line, is a bustling city that long has anchored the automotive industry in Wisconsin. It also is the home of Carthage College and the nearby University of Wisconsin-Parkside campus.

Below: Uniform rows of fruit trees march around a farm and off to the horizon in Door County.

Facing page: The golds, reds and greens of autumn ripple from the placid shores of Gander Lake near the town of Lake Nebagamon in Douglas County.

Above: Mobile home geometry in a subdivision at Schofield, south of Wausau.

Right: Eagle River draws thousands of winter sports enthusiasts each year for World Championship Snowmobile Races.

Facing page: Stately homes reflect the hometown, midwestern feeling of a Milwaukee neighborhood.

Overleaf: Gleaming in the rising sun, Lake Wisconsin stretches along the southern edges of Sauk and Columbia counties.

Above: Looking a bit like Florida from the air, this Oshkosh neighborhood is laced with canals that lead to Lake Winnebago.

Top: Wisconsin is a recreational paradise where water sports are almost a way of life. This marina in Sturgeon Bay is typical of the hundreds of such facilities that dot waterfronts across the state.

Timms Hill, the highest point in Wisconsin, rises high above the surrounding lakes and forests. Rib Mountain near Wausau was often thought of as the highest peak in the state at 1,924 feet, but Timms Hill—southeast of Prentice in Price County—beats it by 28 feet.

Above: Autumn comes early to Rock Island in Lake Michigan, northeast of Washington Island.

Right: The White River snakes its way through the wildlife-rich Bibon Marsh in Bayfield County between Ashland and Drummond.

Above: Ski runs thread their way down the slopes of a ski area near Baraboo.

Right: Squeezing through a bridge opening on ice-locked Sturgeon Bay.

Preceding spread: Hilltop farms peek through a quilt of fog east of La Crosse.

Left: Stevens Point has come to be known as one of the most enticing cities in Wisconsin, with recreation close at hand and a highly respected unit of the University of Wisconsin at its heart.

Below: The rugged Roche-A-Cri butte is one of the most spectacular sights in Roche-A-Cri State Park near Friendship in Adams County. The 300-foot-high sandstone bluff, once an island in a glacial lake, anchors the 400-acre state park.

Thunderstorms build over Lake Michigan off Wind Point, Racine County.

Left: Yerkes Observatory at Williams Bay on Lake Geneva is part of the University of Chicago's Department of Astronomy and Astrophysics. Completed in 1897, it continues to be an active research center exploring the universe. The 90-foot dome, one of the largest of its kind, houses a 40-inch refractor, the world's biggest lens-type telescope.

Below: Slicing his way through seemingly endless fields of grain near Fox Lake.

Above: The setting sun peeks through storm clouds and rain west of Racine.

Facing page: Milwaukee stands as a metropolitan masterpiece on the southwestern shore of Lake Michigan, an ethnic melting pot that grew with the influx of immigrants from around the world. Each ethnic group brought its unique cuisine to help create Milwaukee's great restaurants. The city is, however, perhaps best known for the Three B's: breweries, baseball and basketball.

Facing page: The action never stops in Wisconsin, even in the depths of the winter. Ice racing takes over on Lake Wissota near Chippewa Falls, where autos slip and slide at break-neck speeds around an oval track plowed out of the snow.

Left: Breathtaking beauty and absolute solitude surround the Pilot Island lighthouse.

Below: Fountain City nestled along Highway 35 between the autumn-tinted bluffs of western Wisconsin and the Mississippi River. The city overlooks the Upper Mississippi River National Wildlife and Fish Refuge.

Minocqua is deep in the heart of Wisconsin's northwoods country, famous for crystal-clear lakes and world-class fishing. The resort city is surrounded by Lake Minocqua and Lake Kawaguesaga.

Heading into the rising sun out of the port of Green Bay.

Facing page: An elaborate windbreak near Spooner.

Right: A rainbow of autumn colors covers the hills and encircles farm fields east of La Crosse. The area along the Mississippi River is one of the prime spots in Wisconsin for viewing fall colors.

Below: The heartland of Wisconsin near Wausau turns to gold each fall.

A freighter steams from Lake Michigan into Sturgeon Bay.

Preceding spread: A lone boater creates swirls across an unusually still
Lake Superior at Quarry Point.

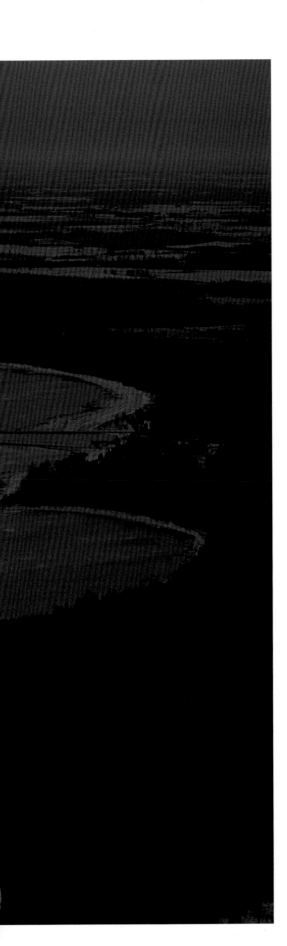

Left: Mounds of taconite ore create an artistic pattern in the snow at Superior.

Below: Highway 53 slips through snow-covered fields and around forests between Blair and Galesville in Trempealeau County.

Lambeau Field glows with lights and fans who flock to Green Bay for a Packers game.

Above: Washington and Rock islands off the northern tip of Door County. Rock Island State Park is accessible only by boat or ferry from Washington Island or Gills Rock, and offers primitive camping, swimming and boating.

Left: The Sturgeon Bay Ship Canal cuts across Door County, providing a water route between Green Bay and Lake Michigan. The city of Sturgeon Bay hugs the shoreline on the both sides of the canal.

Facing page: As autumn moves across the land, Wisconsin's northern hardwood forests turn brilliant with color.

Beavers' handiwork in a pond near Trego, Washburn County.

Facing page, bottom: The lighthouse on Devil's Island sits
on a remote, wind- and snow-swept spit of land far out in Lake
Superior's Apostle Islands.

Left: Hockey players slash and slide across outdoor rinks in Madison.

Facing page: The sheer beauty of Wisconsin is captured in this scene of farms and woodlands west of Tomahawk in Lincoln County.

Left: Lake Winnebago, the largest lake in Wisconsin, provides year-round recreation for the residents of Fond du Lac and other communities along its spectacular shoreline.

Below: Lake Chippewa.

Overleaf: On your marks for the Birkebeiner cross-country ski race, held at Cable near Mount Telemark each February. It's one of North America's largest such events.

Right: A concrete cloverleaf overlaid on fields of green marks the junction of Interstate 90 and Highway 151 near Madison.

Below: Wisconsin has thousands of miles of rivers and streams, and each waterway has its own captivating character. The Flambeau River shown here flows southwest out of Turtle Flambeau Flowage in Iron County to join the Chippewa River.

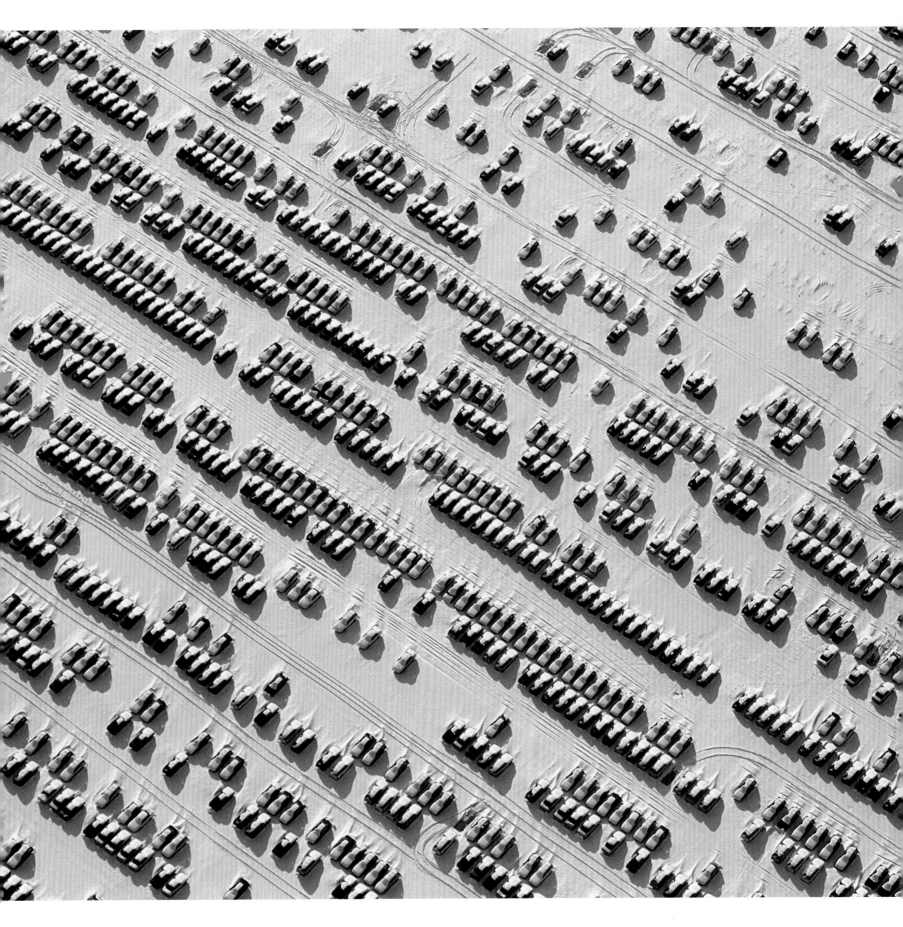

Above: Snow-covered vehicles dot a staging area at Kenosha, where they will be loaded on rail cars for shipment to auto dealers across the country.

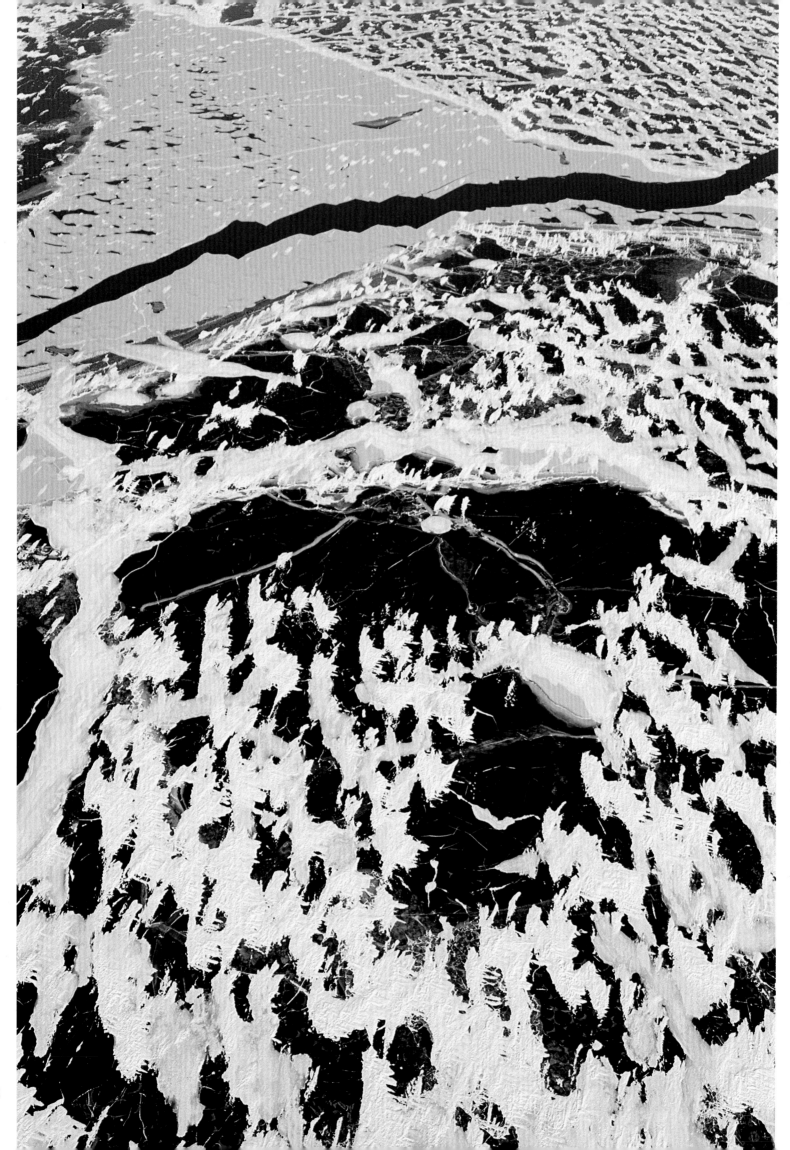

Facing page: Fractured ice turns Green Bay into a winter mosaic.

Left: The city of Lake Geneva nestles into a bay on the lake of the same name. It is one of the most popular spots in southeastern Wisconsin for water sports, recreation, shopping and tourism.

Below: The low-hanging winter sun casts long shadows across America's Dairyland.

Above: Only snow-covered farm fields and woods stand between these winter-locked farms and the frozen shores of Lake Superior. Winter comes early and stays late in the north country east of Superior.

Left: Autumn snow clouds threaten the Wisconsin River near Tomahawk in Lincoln County.

Overleaf: Dawn awakens Chequamegon Bay north of Ashland.